Ramadan: A Dua a Day

By

N. S. Ahmad

بِسْمِ اللَّهِ الرَّحْمَنِ الرَّحِيمِ

And your Lord says:
Call on Me;
I will answer you
Qur'an 40: 60

Index

	Preface	4
Day 1	A dua for increasing productivity	8
Day 2	A dua for times of distress and difficulty	9
Day 3	A dua for uniting the hearts	10
Day 4	A remedy for peer pressure	11
Day 5	A dua for seeking calm amid chaos	12
Day 6	A dua for developing focus	13
Day 7	A dua for inward and outward illumination and protection from bad influences	14
Day 8	A dua for seeking forgiveness, well-being, and divine protection in both worlds	16
Day 9	A defense against spiritual, physical and eternal tribulations	17
Day 10	A dua for the fulfillment of debts, loans, and mortgages	18
Day 11	A dua for seeking Allah's love and proximity	19
Day 12	A dua for having righteous children/for the rectification of children who have gone astray	20
Day 13	A dua for having unwavering faith	21
Day 14	A dua for seeking proper understanding of religion	22
Day 15	A dua for a safe departure from this life with Iman	23
Day 16	A dua for acquiring sincerity and avoiding pretension and hypocrisy	25
Day 17	A dua for asking a healthy fear of Allah	26
Day 18	A dua for bridging differences	28

Day 19	A dua for seeking refuge with Allah from His wrath	29
Day 20	A dua for asking the gift of good character	31
Day 21	a. A dua for paying tribute to parents	33
	b. A dua our Prophet ﷺ frequently made	34
Day 22	A dua for seeking forgiveness for all kinds of sins	35
Day 23	A dua for the rectification of our spiritual frontiers	37
Day 24	A dua for seeking Allah's assistance in each aspect of one's life	39
Day 25	A dua for seeking protection from four disastrous elements	41
Day 26	A dua for developing focus and enhancing memory	43
Day 27	A dua for overcoming disappointment, crushes, and other forms of failures	45
Day 28	A dua for seeking general counsel from Allah in all affairs	46
Day 29	A dua for seeking guidance in this life and full security in the next	48
Day 30	a. A dua for the fulfillment of four overarching needs	51
	b. A dua for retaining firm faith in Allah Most High	52
	Special Moments in Which Supplications are Highly Accepted	53
	A Bouquet of 20 Qur'anic Duas	54

بِسْمِ اللَّهِ الرَّحْمَنِ الرَّحِيمِ

In the Name of Allah, Most Merciful and Compassionate

Preface

The Reality of Dua

Allah Most High says in Surah Ghafir,

وَقَالَ رَبُّكُمُ ادْعُونِي أَسْتَجِبْ لَكُمْ

"And your Lord says: 'Call on Me; I will answer your (Prayer).'" [40:60] Dua (supplication) is a beautiful expression of our servitude to Allah Most High. When we invoke Allah for our needs and share our feelings with Him, it's a sign of our true faith in His existence and reliance on Him alone. It's a sign that Allah Most High has destined good (khair) for us. It's a sign that Allah Most High likes to hear our voices being raised above the heavens. When we act upon the command of Allah "ادعوني", "Call on Me ", we are certain that Allah responds in "استجب لكم", "I will answer you".

The Prophet Salih ﷺ said to his people:

إِنَّ رَبِّي قَرِيبٌ مُجِيبٌ

"My Lord is close and quick to respond."[11:61]

Dua also means drawing near to Allah, going towards Him, while the response from Allah comes in proportion to the frequency of our supplications.

عَنْ أَنَسٍ رضى الله عنه . عَنِ النَّبِيِّ صلى الله عليه وسلم يَرْوِيهِ عَنْ رَبِّهِ، قَالَ " إِذَا تَقَرَّبَ الْعَبْدُ إِلَيَّ شِبْرًا تَقَرَّبْتُ إِلَيْهِ ذِرَاعًا، وَإِذَا تَقَرَّبَ مِنِّي ذِرَاعًا تَقَرَّبْتُ مِنْهُ بَاعًا، وَإِذَا أَتَانِي مَشْيًا أَتَيْتُهُ هَرْوَلَةً ".

Anas (May Allah be pleased with him) reported from the Prophet ﷺ in what he reported from his Lord, the Mighty and Majestic, "When the slave comes towards Me a hand-span, I go an arm-length towards him. When he comes towards Me an arm-length, I go a fathom towards him. When he comes towards Me walking, I go towards him running." [al-Bukhari]

Furthermore, the frequency of our dua never decreases in the treasures of Allah. A part of a long Hadith Qudsi narrated by Imam Muslim on the authority of Abu Dharr al-Ghifari (May Allah be pleased with him) says:

يَا عِبَادِي: لَوْ أَنَّ أَوَّلَكُمْ وَآخِرَكُمْ وَإِنْسَكُمْ وَجِنَّكُمْ قَامُوا فِي صَعِيدٍ وَاحِدٍ فَسَأَلُونِي، فَأَعْطَيْتُ كُلَّ وَاحِدٍ مَسْأَلَتَهُ، مَا نَقَصَ ذَلِكَ مِمَّا عِنْدِي إِلَّا كَمَا يَنْقُصُ الْمِخْيَطُ إِذَا أُدْخِلَ الْبَحْرَ.

"O, My slaves! If the first and the last of you, the human of you and the jinn of you, were to stand in a single place and ask of Me, and were I to give everyone what he requested, that would not decrease what I have, any more than a needle decreases the sea if put into it." [Muslim]

The miraculous power of supplication is evident throughout the Qur'an. Zakariya ﷺ was granted a son despite old age and a barren wife just because he called out to his Lord in secret. The desolate, barren land of Mecca turned into a fully populous one with the dua of Ibrahim ﷺ. Yunus ﷺ was brought forth from the belly of the fish with his sincere invocation. Health, wealth and family were restored to Ayyub ﷺ with the miracle of dua.

The Reason Behind this Compilation

When the blessed month of Ramadan dawns on us, every believer experiences a spiritual uplift and feels motivated to do some extra acts of worship. In addition to fasting and praying the obligatory prayers, every believer endeavors to spend some time in the recitation of the Qur'an, optional prayers, and dhikr. Since the supplications during fasting, in particular, are accepted, we tend to invoke Allah with devotion and enthusiasm especially before Iftar.

عن أنس بن مالك . رضي الله عنه . قال: قال رسول الله صلى الله عليه وسلم: ثلاث دعوات لا ترد: دعوة الوالد لولده، ودعوة الصائم، ودعوة المسافر

Anas bin Malik (May Allah be pleased with him) narrates that the Messenger of Allah ﷺ said, "There are three supplications that are never rejected: The supplication of a father for his child, the supplication of a traveler and the supplication of a fasting person." [Al Baihaqi]

In Ramadan 2017, Allah Most High enabled me to pick a dua from the Qur'anic or Prophetic supplications each day and to share it on social media outlets in both Arabic and English. Upon doing this, one of my friends requested that I compile them all into a publication. My intention was to provide one dua every day so that the readers could focus and persist on it throughout the day especially at the time of suhur and iftar. As we are required to invoke Allah Most High in humility, which is manifested in our begging before Him and lingering at His door. Allah Most High says:

$$ ٱدۡعُواْ رَبَّكُمۡ تَضَرُّعًا وَخُفۡيَةً $$

"Invoke your Lord with humility and in secret." [7:55]

Abu Huraira (May Allah be pleased with him) reported Allah's Messenger ﷺ as saying:

"When one of you makes a supplication (to his Lord) one should not say: 'O Allah, forgive me if You wish, but one should be firm in his asking and should persistently express his desire. Nothing is too great for Allah Most High to give him.'" [Muslim]

We also need to remember how easy it is for Allah to fulfill our needs. The Quran says:

$$ إِنَّمَآ أَمۡرُهُ إِذَآ أَرَادَ شَيۡئًا أَن يَقُولَ لَهُ كُن فَيَكُونُ $$

"Verily, when He intends a thing, His command is "Be" and it is." [36:82]

After much deliberation, I decided to compile them all with the intention that people would find solutions to their problems and they would seek solace and comfort in these Prophetic words. It would bring great pleasure to my heart if this compilation is of any help to those in distress. Besides, these duas should be recited throughout the year and to be kept in our daily routine as souvenirs from the blessed month of Ramadan. These are the 30 duas that follow.

In addition, arranged is a bouquet of various Quranic supplications that can be recited at leisure time or at special moments in which duas are highly accepted such as the moments before dawn, at the end of every obligatory prayer, on the Night of Power, during the rain, etc.

Finally, I want to thank Ruheena Razvi and Ayesha Sultana and Mubeen Husain for editing, proofreading, and giving valuable suggestions. The experience of re-exploring the books of ahadith in order to confirm the words of each dua along with its possible implications was phenomenal for me. I am grateful to Allah Most High for enabling me to use my time and energy in collecting these divine means of communication.

I ask Allah Most High to accept this humble endeavor, to benefit the readers with this compilation, and to make it a beginning of strong connection and communication between Allah and His servants. Ameen.

Day 1

اَللَّهُمَّ أَصْلِحْ لِيْ دِيْنِيَ الَّذِيْ هُوَ عِصْمَةُ أَمْرِيْ وَأَصْلِحْ لِيْ دُنْيَايَ الَّتِيْ فِيْهَا مَعَاشِيْ وَأَصْلِحْ لِيْ آخِرَتِيَ الَّتِيْ إِلَيْهَا مَعَادِيْ وَاجْعَلِ الْحَيَاةَ زِيَادَةً لِيْ فِيْ كُلِّ خَيْرٍ وَاجْعَلِ الْمَوْتَ رَاحَةً لِيْ مِنْ كُلِّ شَرٍّ

O Allah! Set right for me my deen in which lies the protection of my affair and set right for me this world in which lies my livelihood and set right for me the Next World where I have to return. Let my life be such that I earn more and more good in it. And let my death be a joyful release from all troubles.
[Muslim]

A comprehensive supplication for seeking goodness and increasing productivity in both worldly and eternal affairs. A gift for those who want to get rid of the habit of wasting time.

Day 2

لَا إِلَهَ إِلَّا اللَّهُ الْحَلِيْمُ الْكَرِيْمُ سُبْحَانَ اللَّهِ رَبِّ الْعَرْشِ الْعَظِيمِ اَلْحَمْدُ لِلَّهِ رَبِّ الْعَالَمِينَ أَسْأَلُكَ مُوْجِبَاتِ رَحْمَتِكَ وَعَزَائِمَ مَغْفِرَتِكَ وَالْغَنِيمَةَ مِنْ كُلِّ بِرٍّ وَالسَّلَامَةَ مِنْ كُلِّ إِثْمٍ لَا تَدَعْ لِي ذَنْبًا إِلَّا غَفَرْتَهُ وَلَا هَمًّا إِلَّا فَرَّجْتَهُ وَلَا حَاجَةً هِيَ لَكَ رِضًا إِلَّا قَضَيْتَهَا يَا أَرْحَمَ الرَّاحِمِينَ

None has the right to be worshiped but Allah.
Al-Halim (the Forbearing) Al-Karim (the Generous).
Glorious is Allah, Lord of the Magnificent Throne. All
praise is due to Allah, Lord of the worlds. I ask You
for all the means that ensure Your mercy, and that
which will determine Your forgiveness, and a full
share in every virtuous deed, and grant me
complete protection from committing any sins; do
not leave a single sin of mine without forgiving it,
nor a worry without relieving it. Or a need that
pleases you without granting it. O Most-Merciful of
those who show mercy. [Jami` at-Tirmidhi]

It is a very powerful supplication for difficult times and a remedy for
distress.

Day 3

اَللّٰهُمَّ أَلِّفْ بَيْنَ قُلُوبِنَا وَأَصْلِحْ ذَاتَ بَيْنِنَا وَاهْدِنَا سُبُلَ السَّلَامِ وَنَجِّنَا مِنَ الظُّلُمَاتِ إِلَى النُّورِ وَجَنِّبْنَا الْفَوَاحِشَ مَا ظَهَرَ مِنْهَا وَمَا بَطَنَ وَبَارِكْ لَنَا فِيْ أَسْمَاعِنَا وَأَبْصَارِنَا وَقُلُوبِنَا وَأَزْوَاجِنَا وَذُرِّيَّاتِنَا وَتُبْ عَلَيْنَا إِنَّكَ أَنْتَ التَّوَّابُ الرَّحِيْمُ وَاجْعَلْنَا شَاكِرِينَ لِنِعْمَتِكَ مُثْنِينَ بِهَا قَابِلِيْهَا وَأَتِمَّهَا عَلَيْنَا

O Allah! Unite our hearts with love for each other and remove any grievance that we may have against one another, and show us the path of peace. Grant us the light (of guidance) so that we may be liberated from darkness (of ignorance). Protect us from indecency whether open or secret. Bless our hearing, our sight, and our hearts and bless our spouses and our children. And accept our repentance, for You are the Most Forgiving and the Most Merciful. Let us always be grateful to You for Your bounty and Your blessings. Let us accept them in gratitude and let us praise You in abundance for them. And give us all your blessings and favors in full. [Sunan Abi Dawud]

A beautiful supplication for cultivating love, mercy, and peace among ourselves and those around us, Muslims and Non-Muslims. A remedy for hatred. A protection from all forms of indecency. A token of happiness in both worlds.

Day 4

اَللَّهُمَّ احْفَظْنِي بِالْإِسْلَامِ قَائِمًا وَاحْفَظْنِي بِالْإِسْلَامِ قَاعِدًا وَاحْفَظْنِي بِالْإِسْلَامِ رَاقِدًا وَلَا تُشْمِتْ بِي عَدُوًّا وَلَا حَاسِدًا اَللَّهُمَّ إِنِّي أَسْأَلُكَ مِنْ كُلِّ خَيْرٍ خَزَائِنُهُ بِيَدِكَ وأَعُوذُ بِكَ مِنْ كُلِّ شَرٍّ خَزَائِنُهُ بِيَدِكَ

O Allah! Protect me by keeping me steadfast in my faith and let me follow Islam at all times, whether I am standing, sitting or sleeping. And do not provide an occasion to any enemy or an envious person to ridicule me or to laugh at me. O, Allah! I beg of You all that is good, out of the treasures that are in Your Hands. And I seek Your protection from all evil, for that too, is in Your Hands. [Al Hakim]

A supplication for the protection of faith at all times and a remedy for doubts and confusion in one's heart about religion. This dua enables one to deal with peer pressure as well. It can also serve as a chaperone for our youth.

Day 5

اَللَّهُمَّ إِنِّيْ أَسْأَلُكَ رَحْمَةً مِنْ عِنْدِكَ تَهْدِيْ بِهَا قَلْبِيْ وَتَجْمَعُ بِهَا أَمْرِيْ وَتَلُمُّ بِهَا شَعَثِيْ وَتُصْلِحُ بِهَا غَائِبِيْ وَتَرْفَعُ بِهَا شَاهِدِيْ وَتُزَكِّيْ بِهَا عَمَلِيْ وَتُلْهِمُنِيْ بِهَا رَشَدِيْ وَتَرُدُّ بِهَا أُلْفَتِيْ وَتَعْصِمُنِيْ بِهَا مِنْ كُلِّ سُوءٍ

O Allah! I seek Your special mercy to guide my heart with it, and gather my affair with it, and organize that which has been scattered of my affairs with it, and correct that which is hidden from me with it, and elevate that which is apparent from me with it, and purify my actions with it, and inspire my intellect with it, and return my affection with it, and to protect me from all evil with it. [Jami` at-Tirmidhi]

A comprehensive dua for seeking an illuminated heart, mind, and a lifestyle free of chaos. Through these words, one resigns all his/her affairs to Allah and thus attains complete trust in Him.

Day 6

اَللّٰهُمَّ اجْعَلْ وَسَاوِسَ قَلْبِىْ خَشْيَتَكَ وَ ذِكْرَكَ وَ اجْعَلْ
هِمَّتِىْ وَ هَوَايَ فِيْمَا تُحِبُّ وَ تَرْضَى

O Allah! Let all thoughts of my mind and my heart be filled with Your fear and Your remembrance. And let my energies and desires be spent in those deeds that You like and those that will please You. [Al Hizbul A'zam by Mulla Ali al-Qari]

This dua is best for seeking protection against one's thoughts from evil and to develop a focus on what pleases Allah. A shield from all forms of distraction.

Day 7

اللَّهُمَّ اجْعَلْ لِي نُوْرًا فِي قَبْرِيْ وَنُوْرًا فِي قَلْبِيْ وَنُوْرًا مِنْ بَيْنِ يَدَىَّ وَنُوْرًا مِنْ خَلْفِيْ وَنُوْرًا عَنْ يَمِيْنِيْ وَنُوْرًا عَنْ شِمَالِيْ وَنُوْرًا مِنْ فَوْقِيْ وَنُوْرًا مِنْ تَحْتِيْ وَنُوْرًا فِي سَمْعِيْ وَنُوْرًا فِي بَصَرِيْ وَنُوْرًا فِي شَعْرِيْ وَنُوْرًا فِي بَشَرِيْ وَنُوْرًا فِي لَحْمِيْ وَنُوْرًا فِي دَمِيْ وَنُوْرًا فِي عِظَامِيْ اللَّهُمَّ أَعْظِمْ لِيْ نُوْرًا وَأَعْطِنِيْ نُوْرًا وَاجْعَلْ لِيْ نُوْرًا

O Allah! Bring light into my grave, light into my heart, light in front of me, light behind me, light on my right, light on my left, light above me and light below me, light into my hearing, light into my sight, light into my hair, light into my skin, light into my flesh, light into my blood, light into my bones. O, Allah! Increase me with light, grant me light, appoint for me a light. [Jami` at-Tirmidhi]

A dua for inward and outward illumination and protection from bad influences.

.

Note: Allah Most high says:

اللَّهُ وَلِيُّ ٱلَّذِينَ آمَنُوا يُخْرِجُهُم مِّنَ ٱلظُّلُمَٰتِ إِلَى ٱلنُّورِ

"Allah is the Protecting Guardian of those who believe. He brings them out of darkness into light." [2:257]

The world that we live in is the world of shadows (darkness) that veils us to truly witness Allah's oneness and distracts us from remembering Him and submitting to Him alone. The Qur'an says:

اللَّهُ نُورُ ٱلسَّمَٰوَاتِ وَٱلْأَرْضِ

"Allah is the Light of the heavens and the earth." [24:35]

Since the only source of light is Allah Most High Himself, through this dua we ask Him to illuminate our surroundings. We ask Him to dignify our entire body inwardly and outwardly with His divine light that energizes our limbs to perform good actions and fortifies them against evil.

Day 8

اَللَّهُمَّ إِنِّيْ أَسْأَلُكَ الْعَفْوَ وَالْعَافِيَةَ فِي الدُّنْيَا وَالْآخِرَةِ اَللَّهُمَّ إِنِّيْ أَسْأَلُكَ الْعَفْوَ وَالْعَافِيَةَ فِي دِيْنِيْ وَدُنْيَاىَ وَأَهْلِيْ وَمَالِيْ اَللَّهُمَّ اسْتُرْ عَوْرَاتِيْ وَآمِنْ رَوْعَاتِيْ وَاحْفَظْنِيْ مِنْ بَيْنِ يَدَيَّ وَمِنْ خَلْفِيْ وَعَنْ يَمِيْنِيْ وَعَنْ شِمَالِيْ وَمِنْ فَوْقِيْ وَأَعُوْذُ بِعَظَمَتِكَ أَنْ أُغْتَالَ مِنْ تَحْتِيْ

O Allah! I ask You for forgiveness and well-being in this world and in the Hereafter. O Allah, I ask You for forgiveness and well-being in my religious and my worldly affairs. O Allah, conceal my faults, calm my fears, and protect me from my front, my rear, from my right and my left, and from above me, and I seek refuge in Your magnificence in the event that I may suddenly be destroyed from beneath. [Sunan Ibn Majah, Sunan Abi Dawud]

This is a powerful supplication for seeking forgiveness, well-being, and divine protection in both worlds. The crucial need to recite this dua can be understood in our context when we find ourselves and our loved ones in constant exposure to radiation from Wifi and cellular phones. When the mental and spiritual well-being is at stake due to the negative effects of social media (including cyberbullying and internet depression), this dua connects us to the All-Merciful, All-Encompassing and the Most Forgiving Lord who rejoices over the repentance of His slave more than someone who rejoices after having lost the most precious thing he possesses, then finds it.

Day 9

اَللَّهُمَّ إِنِّي أَعُوذُ بِكَ مِنَ الْكَسَلِ وَالْهَرَمِ وَالْمَغْرَمِ وَالْمَأْثَمِ اَللَّهُمَّ إِنِّي أَعُوذُ بِكَ مِنْ عَذَابِ النَّارِ وَفِتْنَةِ النَّارِ وَعَذَابِ الْقَبْرِ وَشَرِّ فِتْنَةِ الْغِنَى وَشَرِّ فِتْنَةِ الْفَقْرِ وَمِنْ شَرِّ فِتْنَةِ الْمَسِيحِ الدَّجَّالِ اَللَّهُمَّ اغْسِلْ خَطَايَاىَ بِمَاءِ الثَّلْجِ وَالْبَرَدِ وَنَقِّ قَلْبِي مِنَ الْخَطَايَا كَمَا يُنَقَّى الثَّوْبُ الْأَبْيَضُ مِنَ الدَّنَسِ وَبَاعِدْ بَيْنِي وَبَيْنَ خَطَايَاىَ كَمَا بَاعَدْتَ بَيْنَ الْمَشْرِقِ وَالْمَغْرِبِ

O Allah! I seek refuge with You from laziness and senility, sins and debts and from the trial of the grave and the punishment of the grave, and from the trial of the Fire and the punishment of the Fire, and from the evil of the trial of wealth. I seek refuge with You from the trial of poverty and I seek refuge with You from the trial of the False Messiah. O Allah, wash my errors from me with snow and hail. Cleanse my heart of errors as You cleanse the white garment of filth. Put a great distance between me and my errors as You put a distance between the east and the west. [Sahih al-Bukhari]

A defense against spiritual, physical and eternal tribulations.

Day 10

اَللَّهُمَّ اكْفِنِيْ بِحَلَالِكَ عَنْ حَرَامِكَ وَأَغْنِنِيْ بِفَضْلِكَ عَمَّنْ سِوَاكَ

O Allah! Grant me enough of what You have made lawful (Halal) so that I may dispense with what you have made unlawful (Haram), And enable me by Your grace to dispense with all but You. [Jami` at-Tirmidhi]

A dua for seeking assistance from Allah in the fulfillment of debts, loans, and mortgages.

Note: Ali (May Allah be pleased with him) reported that a slave with a contract to buy his freedom came to him and said, "I am unable to fulfill my freedom-contract. Please help me. He said, 'Shall I teach you some words which the Messenger of Allah ﷺ taught me? Even if you had a debt the size of a mountain, Allah would pay it for you. Say: "O Allah, give me enough of what You have made lawful to suffice me from what You have made unlawful and enrich me by Your bounty giving me independence from all other than You.'" [At-Tirmidhi]

Day 11

اَللَّهُمَّ إِنِّيْ أَسْأَلُكَ حُبَّكَ وَحُبَّ مَنْ يُحِبُّكَ وَالْعَمَلَ الَّذِي يُبَلِّغُنِيْ حُبَّكَ اَللَّهُمَّ اجْعَلْ حُبَّكَ أَحَبَّ إِلَيَّ مِنْ نَفْسِيْ وَأَهْلِيْ وَمِنَ الْمَاءِ الْبَارِدِ

O Allah! I ask You for Your love and love for those who love You and for actions which will bring Your love to me. O Allah, make Your love dearer to me than myself, my family and cold water. [Jami` at-Tirmidhi]

A dua for seeking Allah's love and proximity.

Note: Allah's love for His servants is not similar to human love in any way. His love for His servants is expressed in His actions such as showing His favor and bounty to His slave or showing His slave special care by protecting him and drawing him close.

As for the servant's love for Allah, it is expressed initially in his submission to Him, in his seeking Allah's pleasure and in avoiding all that displeases Him. A servant's love for Allah can also be defined as tenderness in the heart that leads to a desire to please Allah and to purify the heart from sins.

Day 12

رَبِّ أَوْزِعْنِي أَنْ أَشْكُرَ نِعْمَتَكَ الَّتِي أَنْعَمْتَ عَلَيَّ وَعَلَى وَالِدَيَّ وَأَنْ أَعْمَلَ صَالِحًا تَرْضَاهُ وَأَصْلِحْ لِي فِي ذُرِّيَّتِي إِنِّي تُبْتُ إِلَيْكَ وَإِنِّي مِنَ الْمُسْلِمِينَ

O, my Lord! Grant me the ability to be grateful to You for the favors that You have bestowed upon me and upon my parents. And also grant me the ability to perform such acts of virtue that You like. And let my children be of the righteous ones. Surely, I repent before You, and, without any doubt, I am of those who submit before You. [Al-Ahqaf, 46:15]

A dua for having righteous children. This is also a very effective dua for the rectification of children who have gone astray.

Note: Gratitude to Allah is a means for an increase in blessings.
Allah Most High says in the Quran:

لَئِن شَكَرْتُمْ لَأَزِيدَنَّكُمْ

"If you show thanks, I shall certainly increase you." [14:7]

Thanks for blessings means using everything Allah has given us in ways that are pleasing to Him. Through this supplication, we ask Allah to grant us the ability to use His blessings in His pleasure. Since children are also a blessing from Allah, through this dua we ask Allah to enable us to raise them according to His pleasure. We ask Him to make them righteous who recognize Allah to be their Lord, Islam as their religion, and our master Muhammad ﷺ as their Prophet and Messenger.

Day 13

اَللَّهُمَّ إِنِّي أَسْأَلُكَ إِيْمَانًا لَا يَرْتَدُّ، وَنَعِيْمًا لَا يَنْفَدُ، وَمُرَافَقَةَ مُحَمَّدٍ ﷺ فِي أَعْلَى جَنَّةِ الْخُلْدِ

O Allah! Grant me a faith that never wavers, blessings that never end and the close companionship of our Prophet Muhammad ﷺ in the highest level of the Everlasting Paradise. [Ibn Hibban, Al Hakim, Ahmad, At Tabarani]

This dua is read to ensure that our faith remains firm in all circumstances.

Note: A firm faith puts things in their true perspective. Allah Almighty says:

كُلُّ شَيْءٍ هَالِكٌ إِلَّا وَجْهَهُ لَهُ الْحُكْمُ وَإِلَيْهِ تُرْجَعُونَ

"Everything (that exists) is perishing except His Countenance. His is the rule, and to Him, you will return." [28:88]

Unwavering faith allows one to prefer Allah to any other. It means asking if Allah will be pleased before asking if oneself will be pleased. The Prophet ﷺ said, " Whoever has three traits will taste the sweetness of true faith: love of Allah and His messenger above everything else, love for someone for the sake of nothing besides Allah, and to hate to return to disbelief as he would hate to be thrown into the fire". [Al Bukhari]

Day 14

اَللَّهُمَّ رَبَّ جِبْرَائِيلَ وَمِيكَائِيلَ وَإِسْرَافِيلَ فَاطِرَ السَّمَوَاتِ وَالأَرْضِ عَالِمَ الْغَيْبِ وَالشَّهَادَةِ أَنْتَ تَحْكُمُ بَيْنَ عِبَادِكَ فِيْمَا كَانُوْا فِيْهِ يَخْتَلِفُونَ اِهْدِنِي لِمَا اخْتُلِفَ فِيهِ مِنَ الْحَقِّ بِإِذْنِكَ إِنَّكَ تَهْدِيْ مَنْ تَشَاءُ إِلَى صِرَاطٍ مُسْتَقِيمٍ

O Allah, Lord of Jibra'il (Gabriel), Mika'il (Michael), and Israfil; Originator of the heavens and the earth, [and] Knower of the hidden and the seen; surely You will judge between Your servants on the Day of Judgment, in matters on which they differ. (O Allah!) When such differences arise, by Your command, guide me to the truth; because You guide to the straight path whoever You want to. [Muslim]

A dua for seeking proper understanding of religion and a remedy against hatred, enmity, and sectarian thoughts.

Day 15

اَللَّهُمَّ إِنِّي أَعُوذُ بِكَ مِنَ الْهَدْمِ وَأَعُوذُ بِكَ مِنَ التَّرَدِّي وَأَعُوذُ بِكَ مِنَ الْغَرَقِ وَالْحَرَقِ وَالْهَرَمِ وَأَعُوذُ بِكَ أَنْ يَتَخَبَّطَنِي الشَّيْطَانُ عِنْدَ الْمَوْتِ وَأَعُوذُ بِكَ أَنْ أَمُوتَ فِي سَبِيلِكَ مُدْبِرًا وَأَعُوذُ بِكَ أَنْ أَمُوتَ لَدِيْغًا

O Allah! I seek Your protection from being buried under the debris of a building, or from something else falling down on me; or that I should fall down from any building etc. I seek Your protection from being drowned in water, from being burnt to death and from the difficulties of old age. O Allah! I seek Your protection from being deceived and misled by the devil at the time of my death. And I seek Your protection from dying in Your path while retreating. And I seek Your protection from dying of the sting of a venomous creature. [Sunan Abi Dawud, Sunan an-Nasa'i]

A dua for a safe departure from this life with Iman.

Note: Death is inevitable and imminent. Allah Most High says:

كُلُّ نَفْسٍ ذَآئِقَةُ ٱلْمَوْتِ وَإِنَّمَا تُوَفَّوْنَ أُجُورَكُمْ يَوْمَ ٱلْقِيَـٰمَةِ فَمَن زُحْزِحَ عَنِ ٱلنَّارِ وَأُدْخِلَ ٱلْجَنَّةَ فَقَدْ فَازَ وَمَا ٱلْحَيَوٰةُ ٱلدُّنْيَآ إِلَّا مَتَـٰعُ ٱلْغُرُورِ

"Every soul will taste of death. And you will be paid on the Day of Resurrection only that which you have fairly earned. Whoever is removed from the Fire and is made to enter paradise, he indeed is triumphant. The life of this world is but comfort of illusion." [3:185]

In Islam, death represents a beginning of the afterlife therefore what really matters is submission and obedience to Allah that entails success in the life after death. Scholars have mentioned that all actions are judged by a person's inward state during his or her last act whether it is submission to Allah or disbelief. At that last moment Satan tries his best to wage a final attack. The Prophet ﷺ sought Allah's protection from all the different ways of sudden death that are mentioned in the dua so that a person may have a chance to gather his thoughts to focus upon Allah. But if a believer dies in any of these cases, it would not mean a bad ending, because a believer is promised reward by Allah for every affliction even **if it is the pricking of a thorn.**

Day 16

اَللَّهُمَّ اجْعَلْ سَرِيْرَتِيْ خَيْرًا مِنْ عَلاَنِيَتِيْ وَاجْعَلْ عَلاَنِيَتِيْ صَالِحَةً اَللَّهُمَّ إِنِّيْ أَسْأَلُكَ مِنْ صَالِحِ مَا تُؤْتِي النَّاسَ مِنَ الْمَالِ وَالْأَهْلِ وَالْوَلَدِ غَيْرِ الضَّالِّ وَلاَ الْمُضِلِّ

O Allah! Make my inner self better and more virtuous than my outer self. And let my outer self improve and become more pious and Virtuous. O, Allah! I beg You to grant me all the blessings that You have bestowed on others, whether it is wealth, or spouse, or children. Let our spouses and children be of the righteous ones and not of those who are on the wrong path. And let them not be of those who lead others astray. [Jami` at-Tirmidhi]

A dua for acquiring sincerity and avoiding pretension and hypocrisy.

Day 17

اَللّٰهُمَّ ارْزُقْنِي عَيْنَيْنِ هَطَّالَتَيْنِ تَشْفِيَانِ الْقَلْبَ بِذُرُوفِ الدَّمْعِ مِنْ خَشْيَتِكَ قَبْلَ أَنْ يَكُونَ الدَّمْعُ دَمًا وَالأَضْرَاسُ جَمْرًا

O Allah! Grant me eyes that weep incessantly out of fear of You. And let these tears heal my heart, well before the arrival of the day when, through sheer fright, tears will turn into blood and the very teeth in our jaws will dry up into little pieces of stone (or become burning embers). [The book of Invocation by At Tabarani]

A dua for asking a healthy fear of Allah.

Note: A healthy fear of Allah is obligatory in Islam. It means that we fear His rank over us. When we recognize Allah's numerous blessings on us and in return realize our shortcomings we fear the justice that we deserve for our sins. Crying does not only release toxins and relieve stress. But if done out of awe or yearning for the mercy of Allah, it washes away the sins and softens the heart. Crying out of fear of Allah is the sunnah of our beloved Prophet ﷺ and his companions.

Anas (May Allah be pleased with him) said, "The Messenger of Allah ﷺ heard something about his Companions and he addressed them, saying, 'The Garden and the Fire were shown to me, and I have never seen the like of this day in respect of good and evil. If you knew what I know, you would laugh little and weep much.' A harder day did not come upon the Companions of the Messenger of Allah than that and they covered their faces and sobbed." [Agreed upon]

Those who fear Allah in this world will be safe from all fears in the hereafter.

A part of a hadith narrated by at-Tirmidhi reads: "No man, who wept out of fear of Allah, will enter the Fire until the milk returns to the breast," which means it's impossible for him to enter fire just as it's impossible for the milk to return to the breast.

Day 18

رَبَّنَا اغْفِرْ لَنَا وَلِإِخْوَانِنَا الَّذِيْنَ سَبَقُوْنَا بِالْإِيْمَانِ وَلَا تَجْعَلْ فِيْ قُلُوبِنَا غِلًّا لِّلَّذِيْنَ آمَنُوْا رَبَّنَا إِنَّكَ رَءُوْفٌ رَّحِيْمٌ

Our Lord! Forgive us, and our brothers who came before us into the Faith and do not place in our hearts, rancor against those who have believed Our Lord! You are indeed Full of Kindness, Most Merciful. [Al-Hashr, 59:10]

A dua for bridging differences, and bringing the hearts together.

Day 19

اَللَّهُمَّ إِنِّي أَعُوذُ بِكَ مِنْ زَوَالِ نِعْمَتِكَ وَتَحَوُّلِ عَافِيَتِكَ وَفُجَاءَةِ نِقْمَتِكَ وَجَمِيعِ سَخَطِكَ

O Allah! I seek refuge with You from Your blessing to me vanishing and Your gift of well-being being altered and the sudden arrival of Your revenge and all forms of Your wrath. [Muslim] [1]

A dua for seeking refuge with Allah from His wrath.

Note: Allah Most High says in the Qur'an:

أَفَأَمِنُوا مَكْرَ ٱللَّهِ فَلَا يَأْمَنُ مَكْرَ ٱللَّهِ إِلَّا ٱلْقَوْمُ ٱلْخَٰسِرُونَ

"Did they then feel secure against the Plan of Allah? None feels secure from the Plan of Allah except the people who are the losers." [7:99]

Despair in Allah's mercy is forbidden. On the contrary, feeling secure from His wrath and punishment is a sin as well. We believe that His mercy overcomes His wrath as He has written over His throne. Through

---

[1]Since the last ten nights of Ramadan begin from the night following the 19th fast, it seems suitable to add here the Prophetic guidelines for the whereabouts of Lailat-ul-Qadr.
A'isha (May Allah be pleased with her) reported that the Messenger of Allah ﷺ said, "Look for Lailat-ul-Qadr (Night of Decree) in the last ten nights of Ramadan." [al-Bukhari]
A'isha (May Allah be pleased with her) said, "I said, 'Messenger of Allah, if I know what night the Night of Power is, what do you think I should say during it?' He said, 'Say: اللَّهُمَّ إِنَّكَ عَفُوٌّ كَرِيمٌ تُحِبُّ الْعَفْوَ فَاعْفُ عَنِّي " O Allah, You are Pardoning and you love pardon, so pardon me. [at-Tirmidhi]
This dua is given under the footnote of each upcoming day because each night could be Lailat-ul-Qadr.

this supplication, we take shelter under Allah's mercy and seek refuge in Him from actions that incur His wrath.

Day 20

اَللّٰهُمَّ أَنْتَ الْمَلِكُ لَا إِلَهَ إِلَّا أَنْتَ إِلَّا أَنَا عَبْدُكَ ظَلَمْتُ نَفْسِيْ وَاعْتَرَفْتُ بِذَنْبِيْ فَاغْفِرْ لِيْ ذُنُوبِيْ جَمِيعًا لَا يَغْفِرُ الذُّنُوبَ إِلَّا أَنْتَ وَاهْدِنِيْ لِأَحْسَنِ الْأَخْلَاقِ لَا يَهْدِيْ لِأَحْسَنِهَا إِلَّا أَنْتَ وَاصْرِفْ عَنِّيْ سَيِّئَهَا لَا يَصْرِفُ عَنِّيْ سَيِّئَهَا إِلَّا أَنْتَ لَبَّيْكَ وَسَعْدَيْكَ وَالْخَيْرُ كُلُّهُ فِي يَدَيْكَ وَالشَّرُّ لَيْسَ إِلَيْكَ أَنَا بِكَ وَإِلَيْكَ تَبَارَكْتَ وَتَعَالَيْتَ أَسْتَغْفِرُكَ وَأَتُوبُ إِلَيْكَ

O Allah! You are the Sovereign and there is none worthy of worship but You. I am Your slave, I have wronged myself and I acknowledge my sin. Forgive me all my sins for no one forgives sins but You. Guide me to the best of qualities for none can guide to the best of them but You. Protect me from bad qualities for none can protect against them but You. I am at Your service, all goodness is in Your hands, and evil is not attributed to You. I rely on You and turn to You, blessed and exalted are You, I seek Your forgiveness and repent to You. [Muslim][2]

A dua for asking the gift of good character.

Note: A'isha (May Allah be pleased with her) said, "I heard the Messenger of Allah ﷺ say, 'A believer will attain by his good character

---

the rank of one who prays during the night and fasts during the day.'
[Abu Dawud]

Good character refers to a set of inward qualities and traits such as humility, sincerity, honesty, patience, generosity, sympathy, courage etc. Since the treasures of goodness are in Allah's hands, we beg Him to adorn us with a good character so that we attain proximity to our beloved Prophet ﷺ on the Day of Resurrection.

Jabir (May Allah be pleased with him) reported that the Messenger of Allah ﷺ said, "Those I love most and those sitting nearest to me on the Day of Rising will be those of you with the best character. Those most hateful to me and the furthest of you from me on the Day of Rising will be the pompous, the braggarts and the arrogant.' They said, 'Messenger of Allah, we know the pompous and the braggarts, but who are the arrogant?' He said, 'The proud.'" [at-Tirmidhi]

Day 21

a. رَبِّ ٱرْحَمْهُمَا كَمَا رَبَّيَانِىْ صَغِيرًا

My Lord! Have mercy on them (i.e. my parents) just as they had mercy on me when they raised me when I was little. [Al-Isra, 17:24][3]

A beautiful dua for paying tribute to parents.

Note: Parents' numerous favors upon children can never be returned. Only Allah can reward them for what they do for their kids. The full context of the verse explains one's etiquette towards his/her parents when they reach old age. The Qur'an says: "Your Lord has decreed that you worship none but Him and that you be dutiful to your parents. Whether one or both of them attain old age in your life, don't say a word of contempt to them, nor repel them, but address them in terms of honor. And, out of compassion, submit yourself before them in humility, and say: 'My Lord! bestow on them Your Mercy as they have brought me up in my childhood.'" [17:24]

This Qur'anic supplication only mentions the early stage of one's life which is childhood. A little child is entirely dependent upon his parents in every aspect of his development. The parents raise him in this vulnerable stage till he becomes strong and independent. Through this dua, we ask Allah to cover our parents with His infinite mercy so that He becomes sufficient for all their needs. And if they become dependent upon us physically or financially, then Allah grants us mercy towards them and tawfeeq to serve them. Since they will depend upon Allah in their life after death, we ask Allah to enshroud them in His mercy in all stages of their afterlife.

---

[3] اللَّهُمَّ إِنَّكَ عَفُوٌّ كَرِيمٌ تُحِبُّ الْعَفْوَ فَاعْفُ عَنِّي

O Allah! You are Pardoning and you love pardon, so pardon me.

b. اَللَّهُمَّ رَبَّنَا آتِنَا فِي الدُّنْيَا حَسَنَةً وَفِي الْآخِرَةِ حَسَنَةً وَقِنَا عَذَابَ النَّارِ

O Allah! Our Lord! Give us good in this world and good in the Hereafter and save us from the torment of the fire. Sahih al-Bukhari [Al Baqarah, 2:201][4]

A dua frequently made by our Prophet ﷺ.

Note: Qatada asked Anas (May Allah be pleased with him) which supplication the Prophet ﷺ frequently made. He said: "The supplication that he (the Prophet) made very frequently is this: 'O Allah, grant us the good in this world and the good in the Hereafter and save us from the torment of Hell-Fire.' He (Qatada) said that whenever Anas had to supplicate he made this very supplication, and whenever he (intended) to make another supplication he (inserted) this very supplication in that." [Muslim]

Anas (May Allah be pleased with him) reported that the Prophet ﷺ visited a person from amongst the Muslims in order to inquire (about his health) who had grown feeble like a baby bird. The Prophet ﷺ said: "Did you supplicate Allah for anything or beg of Him about that? He said: Yes. I used to utter (these words): 'O Allah, whatever You are going to punish me with, in the Hereafter, then hasten it for me in this world.' Thereupon Allah's Messenger ﷺ said: 'Glory be to Allah, you have neither the power nor forbearance to take upon yourself (the burden of His Punishment). Why did you not say this: O Allah, grant us good in the world and good in the Hereafter, and save us from the torment of Fire.' He (the Holy Prophet) made this supplication (for him) and he was all right." {Muslim}

The above narration implies that this supplication contains solutions to all of our worldly and eternal problems and concerns.

---

[4] اللَّهُمَّ إِنَّكَ عَفُوٌّ كَرِيمٌ تُحِبُّ الْعَفْوَ فَاعْفُ عَنِّي
O Allah, You are Pardoning and you love pardon, so pardon me.

Day 22

رَبِّ اغْفِرْ لِيْ خَطِيئَتِيْ وَجَهْلِيْ وَإِسْرَافِيْ فِيْ أَمْرِيْ كُلِّهِ وَمَا أَنْتَ أَعْلَمُ بِهِ مِنِّيْ اللَّهُمَّ اغْفِرْ لِيْ خَطَايَاىَ وَعَمْدِيْ وَجَهْلِيْ وَهَزْلِيْ وَكُلُّ ذَلِكَ عِنْدِيْ اللَّهُمَّ اغْفِرْ لِيْ مَا قَدَّمْتُ وَمَا أَخَّرْتُ وَمَا أَسْرَرْتُ وَمَا أَعْلَنْتُ أَنْتَ الْمُقَدِّمُ وَأَنْتَ الْمُؤَخِّرُ وَأَنْتَ عَلَى كُلِّ شَىْءٍ قَدِيرٌ

O Allah! Forgive me my faults, my ignorance, my immoderation in all of my affairs and what You know best of me in it. O Allah, forgive me my errors, what I do intentionally, my ignorance, and my jest. All of that is with me. O Allah, forgive me for what I did in the past and what I may do in the future, what I conceal and what I make public. You are the One who advances matters and defers them. You have power over all things. [Agreed upon][5]

A comprehensive dua for seeking forgiveness for all kinds of sins.

Note: We should understand that time and space only exist for us. Since Allah Most High is beyond the limits of time and space, His forgiveness and mercy also are timeless. Seeking forgiveness for future sins means asking Allah to protect us and grant us the strength to avoid committing sins in future. And even if we commit sins we ask Allah to grant us sincere repentance that eventually washes away any residue from sins. Most of our sins are forgiven due to other acts of obedience, such as wudu, prayers, salawat upon the Prophet ﷺ, umrah, hajj, etc.

---

[5] اللَّهُمَّ إِنَّكَ عَفُوٌّ كَرِيمٌ تُحِبُّ الْعَفْوَ فَاعْفُ عَنِّي
O Allah, You are Pardoning and you love pardon, so pardon me.

Through this dua, we also ask Allah Most High to grant us tawfeeq for such acts of obedience that keep washing our sins in future.

Day 23

اَللَّهُمَّ اقْسِمْ لَنَا مِنْ خَشْيَتِكَ مَا يَحُولُ بَيْنَنَا وَبَيْنَ مَعَاصِيْكَ وَمِنْ طَاعَتِكَ مَا تُبَلِّغُنَا بِهِ جَنَّتَكَ وَمِنَ الْيَقِينِ مَا تُهَوِّنُ بِهِ عَلَيْنَا مُصِيْبَاتِ الدُّنْيَا وَمَتِّعْنَا بِأَسْمَاعِنَا وَأَبْصَارِنَا وَقُوَّتِنَا مَا أَحْيَيْتَنَا وَاجْعَلْهُ الْوَارِثَ مِنَّا وَاجْعَلْ ثَأْرَنَا عَلَى مَنْ ظَلَمَنَا وَانْصُرْنَا عَلَى مَنْ عَادَانَا وَلَا تَجْعَلْ مُصِيْبَتَنَا فِي دِينِنَا وَلَا تَجْعَلِ الدُّنْيَا أَكْبَرَ هَمِّنَا وَلَا مَبْلَغَ عِلْمِنَا وَلَا تُسَلِّطْ عَلَيْنَا مَنْ لَا يَرْحَمُنَا

O Allah! Grant us Your fear to such an extent that it comes between us and Your disobedience. And grant us Your obedience to such an extent that it causes us to reach Your Paradise. And grant us the certainty that makes the afflictions of the world easy for us. And as long as we live, enable us to use our ears, our eyes and the strength of our bodies to their best advantage, and (even after we die) let the effects remain in this world. And let our vengeance be upon those who have wronged us, and aid us against those who show enmity towards us, and do not make our affliction in our religion, and do not make this world our greatest concern, and do not let us limit our knowledge to this world alone, and do not give power over us to those who will not have mercy on us. [Jami` at-Tirmidhi][6]

A dua for the rectification of our spiritual frontiers.

Note: Ibn 'Umar (May Allah be pleased with him) said, "Rarely would the Messenger of Allah ﷺ rise from where he was sitting without making this supplication." [at-Tirmidhi]

O Allah, You are Pardoning and you love pardon, so pardon me.

Day 24

رَبِّ أَعِنِّيْ وَلَا تُعِنْ عَلَيَّ وَانْصُرْنِيْ وَلَا تَنْصُرْعَلَيَّ وَامْكُرْ لِيْ وَلَا تَمْكُرْ عَلَيَّ وَاهْدِنِيْ وَيَسِّرِ الْهُدَى لِيْ وَانْصُرْنِيْ عَلَى مَنْ بَغَى عَلَيَّ رَبِّ اجْعَلْنِيْ لَكَ شَكَّارًا لَكَ ذَكَّارًا لَكَ رَهَّابًا لَكَ مِطْوَاعًا لَكَ مُخْبِتًا إِلَيْكَ أَوَّاهًا مُنِيْبًا رَبِّ تَقَبَّلْ تَوْبَتِيْ وَاغْسِلْ حَوْبَتِيْ وَأَجِبْ دَعْوَتِيْ وَثَبِّتْ حُجَّتِيْ وَسَدِّدْ لِسَانِيْ وَاهْدِ قَلْبِيْ وَاسْلُلْ سَخِيْمَةَ صَدْرِيْ

My Lord! Aid me and do not aid against me, and grant me victory and do not grant victory over me, plot for me and do not plot against me, guide me and facilitate guidance for me, grant me victory over those who transgress against me. My Lord! Make me ever-grateful to You, ever-remembering of You, ever-fearful of You, ever-obedient to You, ever-humble to You, oft-turning and returning to You. My Lord! Accept my repentance, wash away my sins and accept my prayers. Let my reasoning be strong. Let my tongue be truthful, let my heart be rightly guided, and remove all rancor and ill-will from my heart. [Jami` at-Tirmidhi, Sunan Abi Dawud, Ibn Majah][7]

A dua for seeking Allah's assistance in each aspect of one's life.

اللَّهُمَّ إِنَّكَ عَفُوٌّ كَرِيْمٌ تُحِبُّ الْعَفْوَ فَاعْفُ عَنِّي [7]
O Allah, You are Pardoning and you love pardon, so pardon me.

Note: Through this supplication, we ask Allah Most High to make us a means for the downpour of His mercy. We beg Him to allow the light of guidance enter our heart so that we become strong advocates of Islam. We ask for His divine assistance in warding off all forms of inward and outward evil.

Day 25

اَللَّهُمَّ إِنِّي أَعُوذُ بِكَ مِنْ قَلْبٍ لَا يَخْشَعُ وَدُعَاءٍ لَا يُسْمَعُ وَمِنْ نَفْسٍ لَا تَشْبَعُ وَمِنْ عِلْمٍ لَا يَنْفَعُ أَعُوذُ بِكَ مِنْ هَؤُلَاءِ الْأَرْبَعِ

O Allah! I seek refuge in You from a heart that does not humble itself, and from a supplication that is not heard, and from a soul that is never satisfied, and from a knowledge that does not benefit, that is to say, from these four things. [Jami` at-Tirmidhi, Sunan an-Nasa'i][8]

A dua for seeking protection from four disastrous elements.

Note: A heart that does not humble itself is the one that is not touched by the reminders of Allah, that does not feel peace and tranquility in His remembrance and is described in the Qur'an, "Then woe unto those whose hearts are hardened against remembrance of Allah. Such are in plain error." [39:22]

A supplication which is not heard is the one that either contains any form of disobedience to Allah or leads to severing the bonds of kinship, e.g., asking for success in a theft, or asking for disunity among family members, or for divorce between spouses, etc. A supplication which is not answered is also the one asked by a person who does not avoid haram as mentioned by the Prophet ﷺ. A part of a hadith says: The Prophet ﷺ mentioned [the case] of a man who, having journeyed far, is disheveled and dusty, and who spreads out his hands to the sky saying "O Lord! O Lord!," while his food is haram (unlawful), his drink is

---

[8] اللّٰهُمَّ إِنَّكَ عَفُوٌّ كَرِيمٌ تُحِبُّ الْعَفْوَ فَاعْفُ عَنِّي
O Allah, You are Pardoning and you love pardon, so pardon me.

haram, his clothing is haram, and he has been nourished with haram, so how can [his supplication] be answered? [Muslim]

A soul that is never satisfied is the one that is oblivious of Allah's favors and blessings and thus is never content.

A knowledge that does not benefit is that which is not translated into one's actions, does not purify his/her heart from blameworthy traits and is not transmitted to others.

Day 26

اَللّٰهُمَّ ارْحَمْنِيْ بِتَرْكِ الْمَعَاصِيْ أَبَدًا مَا أَبْقَيْتَنِيْ وَارْحَمْنِيْ أَنْ أَتَكَلَّفَ مَا لَا يَعْنِيْنِيْ وَارْزُقْنِيْ حُسْنَ النَّظَرِ فِيْمَا يُرْضِيْكَ عَنِّيْ اللّٰهُمَّ بَدِيْعَ السَّمَوَاتِ وَالْأَرْضِ ذَا الْجَلَالِ وَالْإِكْرَامِ وَالْعِزَّةِ الَّتِيْ لَا تُرَامُ أَسْأَلُكَ يَا اَللّٰهُ يَا رَحْمَنُ بِجَلَالِكَ وَنُورِ وَجْهِكَ أَنْ تُلْزِمَ قَلْبِيْ حِفْظَ كِتَابِكَ كَمَا عَلَّمْتَنِيْ وَارْزُقْنِيْ أَنْ أَتْلُوَهُ عَلَى النَّحْوِ الَّذِيْ يُرْضِيْكَ عَنِّيْ اَللّٰهُمَّ بَدِيْعَ السَّمَوَاتِ وَالْأَرْضِ ذَا الْجَلَالِ وَالْإِكْرَامِ وَالْعِزَّةِ الَّتِيْ لَا تُرَامُ أَسْأَلُكَ يَا اَللّٰهُ يَا رَحْمَنُ بِجَلَالِكَ وَنُورِ وَجْهِكَ أَنْ تُنَوِّرَ بِكِتَابِكَ بَصَرِيْ وَأَنْ تُطْلِقَ بِهِ لِسَانِيْ وَأَنْ تُفَرِّجَ بِهِ عَنْ قَلْبِيْ وَأَنْ تَشْرَحَ بِهِ صَدْرِيْ وَأَنْ تَغْسِلَ بِهِ بَدَنِيْ لِأَنَّهُ لَا يُعِيْنُنِيْ عَلَى الْحَقِّ غَيْرُكَ وَلَا يُؤْتِيْهِ إِلَّا أَنْتَ وَلَا حَوْلَ وَلَا قُوَّةَ إِلَّا بِاللّٰهِ الْعَلِيِّ الْعَظِيمِ

O Allah! Have mercy on me by enabling me to abandon sins forever as long as You keep me alive. And have mercy on me that I do not take upon myself what does not concern me, and grant me a good insight into what will make You pleased with me. O Allah, Originator of the heavens and the earth, Possessor of glory, and generosity, and honor that is inconceivable, I ask You, O Allah! O Most Merciful One! By Your Majesty and the light of Your Countenance, to make my heart devoted to memorizing Your Book as You taught me, and enable me to recite it in a manner that is pleasing to You. O Allah, Originator of the heavens and the earth, Possessor of glory, and generosity, and honor that is inconceivable, I ask You, O Allah! O Most Merciful One! By Your Majesty and the light of Your Countenance, to enlighten my sight with Your Book, and let the verses of the Quran flow from my tongue, and to relieve my heart with it, and to expand my chest with it, and to wash my body with it because You alone can help me in what is right; and You alone can give me correct guidance. I have neither the ability to do any good nor the strength to avoid any evil unless with the support of Allah, the High, the Magnificent. [Jami` at-Tirmidhi][9]

A supplication for developing focus and enhancing memory in general and seeking Allah's help in memorizing the Qur'an in particular.

---

[9] اللَّهُمَّ إِنَّكَ عَفُوٌّ كَرِيمٌ تُحِبُّ الْعَفْوَ فَاعْفُ عَنِّي

O Allah, You are Pardoning and you love pardon, so pardon me.

Day 27

اَللّٰهُمَّ ارْزُقْنِيْ حُبَّكَ وَحُبَّ مَنْ يَنْفَعُنِيْ حُبُّهُ عِنْدَكَ اللّٰهُمَّ مَا رَزَقْتَنِي مِمَّا أُحِبُّ فَاجْعَلْهُ قُوَّةً لِيْ فِيمَا تُحِبُّ اللّٰهُمَّ وَمَا زَوَيْتَ عَنِّيْ مِمَّا أُحِبُّ فَاجْعَلْهُ لِيْ فَرَاغًا فِيْمَا تُحِبُّ

O Allah! Grant me Your love and the love of those whose love will benefit me with You. O Allah, whatever You have provided me of that which I love, then make it a strength for me for that which You love. O Allah, and what You have withheld from me of that which I love, then turn this void into a desire to do what You love. [Jami` at-Tirmidhi]

A beautiful dua for seeking the ability to use Allah's blessings in ways that are pleasing to Him. Also, a humble expression to seek strength in overcoming disappointment, crushes, and other forms of failures.[10]

---

[10] اللّٰهُمَّ إِنَّكَ عَفُوٌّ كَرِيمٌ تُحِبُّ الْعَفْوَ فَاعْفُ عَنِّي
O Allah, You are Pardoning and you love pardon, so pardon me.

Day 28

اَللَّهُمَّ إِنِّي أَسْأَلُكَ مِنَ الْخَيْرِ كُلِّهِ عَاجِلِهِ وَآجِلِهِ مَا عَلِمْتُ مِنْهُ وَمَا لَمْ أَعْلَمْ وَأَعُوذُ بِكَ مِنَ الشَّرِّ كُلِّهِ عَاجِلِهِ وَآجِلِهِ مَا عَلِمْتُ مِنْهُ وَمَا لَمْ أَعْلَمْ اَللَّهُمَّ إِنِّي أَسْأَلُكَ مِنْ خَيْرِ مَا سَأَلَكَ عَبْدُكَ وَنَبِيُّكَ وَأَعُوذُ بِكَ مِنْ شَرِّ مَا عَاذَ بِهِ عَبْدُكَ وَنَبِيُّكَ اَللَّهُمَّ إِنِّي أَسْأَلُكَ اَلْجَنَّةَ وَمَا قَرَّبَ إِلَيْهَا مِنْ قَوْلٍ أَوْ عَمَلٍ وَأَعُوذُ بِكَ مِنَ النَّارِ وَمَا قَرَّبَ مِنْهَا مِنْ قَوْلٍ أَوْ عَمَلٍ وَأَسْأَلُكَ أَنْ تَجْعَلَ كُلَّ قَضَاءٍ قَضَيْتَهُ لِي خَيْرًا

O Allah! I ask you of all good, whether it is given soon or at a later time, what I know and what I do not know. And I seek refuge in You from all evil, whether it is coming sooner or coming later, what I know and what I do not know. O Allah! I ask of You all good that your servant and Prophet Muhammad ﷺ has asked You for. And I seek refuge in You from all evil that your servant and Prophet Muhammad ﷺ sought refuge in You from. O Allah! I ask You for Paradise and what brings me nearer to it of deeds and words. I seek refuge in You from Hellfire and what brings me near to it of deeds and words. And let every decision You make concerning me, be better for me and in my favor. [Ibn Maja, Ibn Hibban, Al Hakim][11]

---

[11] اللَّهُمَّ إِنَّكَ عَفُوٌّ كَرِيمٌ تُحِبُّ الْعَفْوَ فَاعْفُ عَنِّي
O Allah, You are Pardoning and you love pardon, so pardon me.

A supplication for seeking general counsel and help from Allah in all affairs. Through this dua, we ask Allah to grant us the ability to make right decisions. We beg Him to guide us towards what is good for us and turn us away from what is bad for us. A very comprehensive dua for asking all good and for seeking refuge in Him from all evil.

Day 29

اللَّهُمَّ إِنِّي أُنْزِلُ بِكَ حَاجَتِي وَإِنْ قَصَرَ رَأْيِي وَضَعُفَ عَمَلِي افْتَقَرْتُ إِلَى رَحْمَتِكَ فَأَسْأَلُكَ يَا قَاضِيَ الْأُمُورِ وَيَا شَافِيَ الصُّدُورِ كَمَا تُجِيرُ بَيْنَ الْبُحُورِ أَنْ تُجِيرَنِي مِنْ عَذَابِ السَّعِيرِ وَمِنْ دَعْوَةِ الثُّبُورِ وَمِنْ فِتْنَةِ الْقُبُورِ اللَّهُمَّ مَا قَصَّرَ عَنْهُ رَأْيِي وَلَمْ تَبْلُغْهُ نِيَّتِي وَلَمْ تَبْلُغْهُ مَسْأَلَتِي مِنْ خَيْرٍ وَعَدْتَهُ أَحَدًا مِنْ خَلْقِكَ أَوْ خَيْرٍ أَنْتَ مُعْطِيهِ أَحَدًا مِنْ عِبَادِكَ فَإِنِّي أَرْغَبُ إِلَيْكَ فِيهِ وَأَسْأَلُكَهُ بِرَحْمَتِكَ رَبَّ الْعَالَمِينَ اللَّهُمَّ ذَا الْحَبْلِ الشَّدِيدِ وَالْأَمْرِ الرَّشِيدِ أَسْأَلُكَ الْأَمْنَ يَوْمَ الْوَعِيدِ وَالْجَنَّةَ يَوْمَ الْخُلُودِ مَعَ الْمُقَرَّبِينَ الشُّهُودِ الرُّكَّعِ السُّجُودِ الْمُوفِينَ بِالْعُهُودِ إِنَّكَ رَحِيمٌ وَدُودٌ وَأَنْتَ تَفْعَلُ مَا تُرِيدُ اَللَّهُمَّ اجْعَلْنَا هَادِينَ مُهْتَدِينَ غَيْرَ ضَالِّينَ وَلَا مُضِلِّينَ سِلْمًا لِأَوْلِيَائِكَ وَعَدُوًّا لِأَعْدَائِكَ نُحِبُّ بِحُبِّكَ مَنْ أَحَبَّكَ وَنُعَادِي بِعَدَاوَتِكَ مَنْ خَالَفَكَ اَللَّهُمَّ هَذَا الدُّعَاءُ وَعَلَيْكَ الْإِسْتِجَابَةُ وَهَذَا الْجَهْدُ وَعَلَيْكَ التُّكْلَانُ

O Allah! I place my need before You, although my understanding is limited, and my actions are weak. I am in need of Your mercy, so I ask You, O You who decides all matters and heals the hearts, as You separate the seas from mixing, in the same way, protect me from the fire of Hell and from the cry for destruction (in order to get rid of the punishment), and from the trial of the graves.

O Allah! Whatever my mind has not been able to conceive, and my intention and desire has not reached, of good that You have promised to anyone from Your creation, or any good You are going to give to any of Your slaves, then indeed, I seek it from You and I ask You for it, by Your mercy, O Lord of the Worlds.

O Allah! The Owner of the strong covenant and the Director to the right path, I ask You for security on the Day of Torment; and Paradise on the Day of Eternity along with (Your) close witnesses, those who bow down and prostrate, those who fulfill the covenants. Verily You are Most Merciful and Most Loving. And indeed, You do what You wish.

O Allah! Let us be of those who guide others to the right path and are themselves guided aright; who are neither misguided nor misguide others; who are at peace with Your friends, and at war with Your enemies. We love due to Your love, those who love You, and abhor, due to Your enmity those who oppose You.

O Allah! This is the supplication (from us) and from You is the response, and this the effort (from us), and upon You is the reliance. [Jami` at-Tirmidhi][12]

A dua for seeking guidance in this life and full security in the next.

---

[12] اللَّهُمَّ إِنَّكَ عَفُوٌّ كَرِيمٌ تُحِبُّ الْعَفْوَ فَاعْفُ عَنِّي
O Allah, You are Pardoning and you love pardon, so pardon me.

Note: Since this is the time to bid farewell to Ramadan[13], through this supplication we humbly ask Allah to grant us every good that is in His knowledge but is beyond our perception. After fasting the whole month for His sake, reciting His word, and performing extra prayers for His sake, this is a befitting moment to ask Him to grant us security at every stage in the hereafter and guidance in this world.

---

[13] Ramadan could be of 29 days. In that case, it would be the end of Ramadan.

Day 30

a. اَللَّهُمَّ إِنِّيْ أَسْأَلُكَ الْهُدَى وَالتُّقَى وَالْعَفَافَ وَالْغِنَى

O, Allah! I ask You for guidance, fearful awareness, chastity, and independence. [Muslim][14]

A dua for the fulfillment of four overarching needs.

Note: This short yet comprehensive supplication covers four most crucial needs of a believer. First, we ask Allah for Guidance which is an illumination in the heart that reminds us of the purpose of this temporary life and uplifts us to prepare for the next world. After this, we realize that we are surrounded by distractions; therefore, we ask Allah Most High for a constant awareness of Him that protects us from disobedience. With regard to the creation, we want to respect the boundaries set by the Creator in our social interactions; therefore, we ask Him for chastity. Asking for chastity also implies asking for facilitation in marriage since it is the institution for preserving chastity. Then we ask Allah to enrich us outwardly and inwardly, and make us financially independent of everyone and everything except Him so that we do not ask others or want what they have.

---

[14] اللَّهُمَّ إِنَّكَ عَفُوٌّ كَرِيمٌ تُحِبُّ الْعَفْوَ فَاعْفُ عَنِّي

O Allah, You are Pardoning and you love pardon, so pardon me.

b. يَا مُقَلِّبَ الْقُلُوْبِ ثَبِّتْ قَلْبِيْ عَلَى دِيْنِكَ

O Turner of the hearts! Make my heart firm in Your religion. [Jami` at-Tirmidhi]

A dua for retaining firm faith in Allah.

Note: Hearts of the creation are under the ultimate power of Allah and He turns them however He wants. He can still create a Moses in the house of Pharaoh, Ibrahim in the house of idols, as well as Kan'an in the house of Nuh[15]. The only way to ensure that our faith remains firm upon Islam is to turn to the Turner of the hearts.

Anas (May Allah be pleased with him) narrated:
"The Messenger of Allah ﷺ would often say: 'O Changer of the Hearts! Strengthen my heart upon Your Religion. So I said: 'O Prophet of Allah! We believe in you and what you have brought, but do you fear for us?' He said: 'Yes. Indeed the hearts are between two Fingers of Allah's Fingers, He changes them as He wills.'" [at-Tirmidhi]

---

[15] Allama Al-Qurtubi has mentioned that the son of Nuh ﷺ who was drowned in the storm was Kan'an.

Special Moments in Which Supplications are Highly Accepted

1. During the third portion of the night, especially prior to dawn (at the time of Suhur).
2. In the prostration of (optional) prayers. However, it is preferred to supplicate through the Qur'anic and Prophetic supplications inside the prayer.
3. The period between adhan (call to prayer) and iqama (call to commence prayer).
4. After the completion of obligatory prayers.
5. On the night preceding Friday (Friday's eve).
6. During the "Moment of Acceptance" on Friday, which is differed upon among scholars. Some say it is between the time when the imam gets up for the sermon until the completion of the Friday prayer. Some say it is between Asr prayer and sunset, while others say it is just moments before sunset.
7. On the Night of Qadr.
8. After completing the Qur'an.
9. When a Muslim supplicates for his brother/sister in his/her absence.
10. While drinking the water of Zam Zam.

A Bouquet of Qur'anic Duas

١. رَبَّنَا تَقَبَّلْ مِنَّا إِنَّكَ أَنْتَ ٱلسَّمِيعُ ٱلْعَلِيمُ وَتُبْ عَلَيْنَآ إِنَّكَ أَنْتَ ٱلتَّوَّابُ ٱلرَّحِيمُ

Our Lord! Accept (this service) from us; for You are the All-Hearing, the All-Knowing. And accept our repentance. Truly, You are the One Who accepts repentance, the Most Merciful. [2:127, 128]

٢. رَبَّنَا عَلَيْكَ تَوَكَّلْنَا وَإِلَيْكَ أَنَبْنَا وَإِلَيْكَ ٱلْمَصِيرُ رَبَّنَا لَا تَجْعَلْنَا فِتْنَةً لِّلَّذِينَ كَفَرُوا وَٱغْفِرْ لَنَا رَبَّنَا إِنَّكَ أَنتَ ٱلْعَزِيزُ ٱلْحَكِيمُ

Our Lord, in You (Alone) we put our trust, and to You (Alone) we turn in repentance, and to You (Alone) is (our) final return. Our Lord, do not expose us to mistreatment (at the hands of) the disbelievers, and forgive us. Our Lord, You are indeed the Mighty, the Wise. [60: 4,5]

٣. رَبَّنَا لَا تُؤَاخِذْنَآ إِنْ نَّسِينَآ أَوْ أَخْطَأْنَا رَبَّنَا وَلَا تَحْمِلْ عَلَيْنَآ إِصْرًا كَمَا حَمَلْتَهُ عَلَى ٱلَّذِينَ مِنْ قَبْلِنَا رَبَّنَا وَلَا تُحَمِّلْنَا مَا لَا طَاقَةَ لَنَا بِهِ وَٱعْفُ عَنَّا وَٱغْفِرْ لَنَا وَٱرْحَمْنَآ أَنتَ مَوْلَانَا فَٱنصُرْنَا عَلَى ٱلْقَوْمِ ٱلْكَافِرِينَ

Our Lord! Do not hold us accountable if we forget or make a mistake and Our Lord, do not place on us such a burden as You have placed on those before us, and, Our Lord, do not make us bear a burden for which we have no strength. And pardon us, and grant us forgiveness, and have mercy on us. You are our Lord, so then help us against the disbelieving people. [2:286]

4. رَبَّنَا لَا تُزِغْ قُلُوْبَنَا بَعْدَ إِذْ هَدَيْتَنَا وَهَبْ لَنَا مِن لَّدُنْكَ رَحْمَةً إِنَّكَ أَنْتَ ٱلْوَهَّابُ رَبَّنَآ إِنَّكَ جَامِعُ ٱلنَّاسِ لِيَوْمٍ لَّا رَيْبَ فِيْهِ إِنَّ ٱللَّهَ لَا يُخْلِفُ ٱلْمِيْعَادَ

Our Lord! Do not let our hearts deviate (from the truth) after You have guided us and grant us mercy from You. Truly, You alone are the One who bestows in abundance. Our Lord! Verily, it is You Who will gather mankind together on the Day about which there is no doubt. Verily, Allah never fails in His Promise. [3:8,9]

5. رَبِّ هَبْ لِيْ مِن لَّدُنْكَ ذُرِّيَّةً طَيِّبَةً إِنَّكَ سَمِيْعُ ٱلدُّعَآءِ

O, my Lord! Grant me from You a progeny that is pure (good); for You are the One who listens to the prayer. [3:38]

6. رَبَّنَآ آمَنَّا بِمَآ أَنزَلْتَ وَٱتَّبَعْنَا ٱلرَّسُوْلَ فَٱكْتُبْنَا مَعَ ٱلشَّاهِدِيْنَ

Our Lord! We believe in what You have revealed, and we follow the Messenger; then write us down among those who bear witness (to the truth i.e. There is no god but Allah). [3:53]

7. رَبَّنَا ٱغْفِرْلَنَا ذُنُوْبَنَا وَإِسْرَافَنَا فِيْ أَمْرِنَا وَثَبِّتْ أَقْدَامَنَا وَٱنْصُرْنَا عَلَى ٱلْقَوْمِ ٱلْكَافِرِيْنَ

Our Lord! Forgive us our sins and our excesses in our conduct, establish our feet firmly and help us against the disbelieving people. [3:147]

8. رَبَّنَآ إِنَّنَا سَمِعْنَا مُنَادِيًا يُّنَادِىْ لِلْإِيْمَانِ أَنْ آمِنُوْا بِرَبِّكُمْ فَآمَنَّا رَبَّنَا فَٱغْفِرْ لَنَا ذُنُوْبَنَا وَكَفِّرْ عَنَّا سَيِّئَاتِنَا وَتَوَفَّنَا مَعَ ٱلْأَبْرَارِ

Our Lord! Verily, we have heard the call of one (Muhammad ﷺ) calling to Faith: 'Believe in your Lord,' and we have believed. Our Lord! Forgive us our sins and expiate from us our evil deeds, and make us die in the company of the righteous. [3:193]

9. رَبَّنَا وَآتِنَا مَا وَعَدتَّنَا عَلَىٰ رُسُلِكَ وَلَا تُخْزِنَا يَوْمَ ٱلْقِيَامَةِ إِنَّكَ لَا تُخْلِفُ ٱلْمِيعَادَ

Our Lord! Grant us what You have promised us through Your Messengers and do not disgrace us on the Day of Resurrection, for You never break (Your) Promise. [3:194]

10. رَبَّنَا ظَلَمْنَآ أَنْفُسَنَا وَإِن لَّمْ تَغْفِرْ لَنَا وَتَرْحَمْنَا لَنَكُوْنَنَّ مِنَ ٱلْخَاسِرِيْنَ

Our Lord! We have wronged ourselves. If You do not forgive us and do not bestow upon us Your Mercy, we shall certainly be of the losers. [7: 23]

11. فَاطِرَ ٱلسَّمَاوَاتِ وَٱلْأَرْضِ أَنْتَ وَلِيِّ فِى ٱلدُّنْيَا وَٱلْأَخِرَةِ تَوَفَّنِى مُسْلِمًا وَّأَلْحِقْنِى بِٱلصَّالِحِيْنَ

O Creator of the heavens and the earth! You are my Protecting Friend in the world and the Hereafter. Make me die as a Muslim, and unite me with the righteous. [12: 101]

12. رَبِّ آجْعَلْنِىْ مُقِيْمَ ٱلصَّلَاةِ وَمِنْ ذُرِّيَّتِىْ رَبَّنَا وَتَقَبَّلْ دُعَآءِ رَبَّنَا آغْفِرْلِىْ وَلِوَالِدَىَّ وَلِلْمُؤْمِنِيْنَ يَوْمَ يَقُوْمُ ٱلْحِسَابُ

O, my Lord! Make me one who establishes regular prayer, and also (raise such) among my offspring. O our Lord! And accept my Prayer. O our Lord! Cover (us) with Your Forgiveness— me, my parents, and (all) Believers, on the Day when the Reckoning will take place. [14:40,41]

13. رَبَّنَآ آتِنَا مِن لَّدُنْكَ رَحْمَةً وَّهَيِّئْ لَنَا مِنْ أَمْرِنَا رَشَدًا

Our Lord! Bestow on us mercy from Yourself, and facilitate guidance for us in our matters. [18:10]

14. رَبِّ آشْرَحْ لِىْ صَدْرِىْ وَيَسِّرْ لِىْ أَمْرِىْ وَآحْلُلْ عُقْدَةً مِّن لِّسَانِىْ يَفْقَهُوْا قَوْلِىْ

My Lord! Expand my chest, and ease my task for me; and loose a knot from my tongue, that they may understand my speech. [20:25]

15. رَبِّ أَعُوْذُ بِكَ مِنْ هَمَزَاتِ ٱلشَّيَاطِيْنِ وَأَعُوْذُ بِكَ رَبِّ أَن يَّحْضُرُوْنِ

My Lord! I seek refuge with You from the whisperings of the shayateen (devils) and I seek refuge in You from their coming near me. [23:97]

16. رَبَّنَا ٱصْرِفْ عَنَّا عَذَابَ جَهَنَّمَ إِنَّ عَذَابَهَا كَانَ غَرَامًا إِنَّهَا سَاءَتْ مُسْتَقَرًّا وَمُقَامًا

Our Lord! Avert from us the wrath of Hell, for its wrath is indeed a persisting affliction. Indeed it is evil as an abode, and a place to rest in. [25:65, 66]

17. رَبَّنَا هَبْ لَنَا مِنْ أَزْوَاجِنَا وَذُرِّيَّاتِنَا قُرَّةَ أَعْيُنٍ وَّٱجْعَلْنَا لِلْمُتَّقِينَ إِمَامًا

Our Lord! Bestow on us from our wives and our offspring the comfort of our eyes, and make us leaders for the pious. [25:74]

18. رَبِّ أَوْزِعْنِيْ أَنْ أَشْكُرَ نِعْمَتَكَ ٱلَّتِيْ أَنْعَمْتَ عَلَيَّ وَعَلَىٰ وَالِدَيَّ وَأَنْ أَعْمَلَ صَالِحًا تَرْضَاهُ وَأَدْخِلْنِيْ بِرَحْمَتِكَ فِيْ عِبَادِكَ ٱلصَّالِحِيْنَ

O, my Lord! Enable me that I may be grateful for Your favors which You have bestowed on me and on my parents and to do good that shall be pleasing to You, and include me in (the number of) Your righteous slaves. [27:19]

19. رَبِّ إِنِّيْ لِمَا أَنْزَلْتَ إِلَيَّ مِنْ خَيْرٍ فَقِيْرٌ

O, my Lord! Truly I am in (desperate) need of any good that You bestow on me. [28:24]

20. رَبَّنَا ٱغْفِرْ لَنَا وَلِإِخْوَانِنَا ٱلَّذِينَ سَبَقُوْنَا بِٱلْإِيْمَانِ وَلَا تَجْعَلْ فِىْ قُلُوْبِنَا غِلاًّ لِّلَّذِيْنَ آمَنُوْا رَبَّنَا إِنَّكَ رَءُوْفٌ رَّحِيْمٌ

Our Lord! Forgive us and our brothers who were before us in the faith, and do not place in our hearts any rancor toward those who believe. Our Lord! You are indeed Full of Kindness, Most Merciful. [59:10]

In closing, I humbly request the readers to also include in their duas the compiler, her parents and other family members, the Nakhlah Institute and all associated with it.

وَآخِرُ دَعْوَانا أَنِ الْحَمْدُ لِلَّهِ رَبِّ الْعَالَمِينَ وصَلَّى اللهُ عَلَى سَيِّدِنَا مُحَمَّدٍ وَّعَلَى آلِهِ وَصَحْبِهِ أَجْمَعِيْنَ

And the conclusion of our prayer is: Praise be to Allah, Lord of the Worlds. May Allah Most High bless our master Muhammad and his family and companions.

N. S. Ahmad
nakhlahusa.org
March 27, 2018

Made in the USA
Middletown, DE
02 April 2022